T0108925

LEIBNIZ IN 90 MINUTES

Leibniz
IN 90 MINUTES

Paul Strathern

IVAN R. DEE
CHICAGO

LEIBNIZ IN 90 MINUTES. Copyright © 2000 by Paul Strathern. All rights reserved, including the right to reproduce this book or portions thereof in any form. For information, address: Ivan R. Dee, Publisher, 1332 North Halsted Street, Chicago 60622. Manufactured in the United States of America and printed on acid-free paper.

Library of Congress Cataloging-in-Publication Data:
Strathern, Paul, 1940–
    Leibniz in 90 minutes / Paul Strathern
      p.   cm. — (Philosophers in 90 minutes)
    Includes bibliographical references and index.
    ISBN 1-56663-330-3 (cloth : alk. paper) — ISBN 1-56663-331-1 (pbk. : alk. paper)
    1. Leibniz, Gottfried Wilhelm, Freiherr von, 1646–1716.
  I. Title: Leibniz in ninety minutes.   II. Title.

B2598 S77 2000
193—dc21   00-056964

Contents

LEIBNIZ IN 90 MINUTES

Introduction

Leibniz was the archetypal caricature genius. He lived a life rich in incidents of high farce, of whose nature he was seldom aware. He knew everything about everything, yet he simply didn't understand how ordinary people thought and behaved. This said, he was certainly one of the more presentable philosophers (though this probably says more about philosophers than about Leibniz). He appeared at courts throughout Europe, where the royals and aristocrats even took him seriously (though this probably says more about the royals and aristocrats . . .). For almost his entire adult life Leibniz was employed by the court at Hanover—and several other courts at the same time. He always took on as many appointments as he could and insisted upon being paid the full salary for these positions. He would become highly indignant when his pay was stopped because his employers had heard he was off working somewhere else.

To list Leibniz's achievements would once again make him sound like a parodic exaggeration of genius. In fact it's impossible to list all his ideas and discoveries, many of which he kept in a trunkload of papers that have yet to be published in their entirety. Fortunately Leibniz is of interest to us mainly as a philosopher. Yet even here the picture remains unclear. Bertrand Russell, who wrote one of the finest critical works on Leibniz's philosophy, was of the opinion that Leibniz had produced two philosophies. The first was a simple philosophy for public consumption: a shallow optimistic metaphysics intended to delight princesses. His other, less optimistic ideas he consigned to his trunk. These were part of a more complex, logical, and profound system which could only be understood with difficulty by minds of the caliber of Leibniz himself (and Russell, of course). Characteristically, both of these philosophies remained unfinished—if indeed they really are two separate philosophies. Most other commentators, not having minds equal to Leibniz or Russell, claim that the simple philosophy and the complex one are really part and parcel of the same thing—which is neither as simple nor as complex as its two parts. Having cleared up these basic points, we may now proceed to Leibniz's life.

Leibniz's Life and Works

His life began, seriously enough, on July 1, 1646, in Leipzig. Three years later came the end of the Thirty Years War, which had swept through Europe and left Germany in a state of devastation. This catastrophe was to cast its shadows over the European political scene for decades to come, in much the same way that the shades of World War II have only recently begun to fade in Eastern Europe.

Leibniz's father, Friedrich Leibnütz, was professor of moral philosophy at Leipzig University. His mother, Catherina, nee Schmuck, was Friedrich's third wife. Their son was christened Gottfried Wilhelm Leibnütz (he was to change the spelling of his family name at the age of twenty). When Leibniz was just five years old his father died, leaving him and a sister to be brought up by their mother. According to all reports Catherina was a great believer in peace and harmony, who never spoke ill of anyone. Normally one would look upon this as a bit of the usual mythology. But in this case it must have been true. Leibniz was deeply affected by his mother and retained these very characteristics of hers to the end of his days. Despite everything (and this everything was to be quite something), Leibniz's life was deeply harmonious. His long-term secretary Eckhart records that he never heard him speak ill of anyone. Leibniz's philosophy too is permeated with a deep sense of harmony, and his lifelong political endeavors were invariably motivated by an attempt to bring harmony to the European scene.

Leibniz did go to school but said that most of his education was conducted at home, reading through his father's library. He always claimed that he was self-taught, and it shows, even at this supreme level of genius. As a boy he read obsessively, following his train of thought as the fancy took him—until the entire floor of the library and all the tables and chairs were covered with opened books. The boy is all too recognizable in the man. In adult life Leibniz was capable of hatching half a dozen brilliant crackpot schemes in a week. These could range from a submarine to an entirely new form of clock, from a revolutionary lantern to a coach as fast as a modern car (when the roads were still only rutted tracks), from a horizontal windmill to a machine for measuring good and evil—none of which would ever be finished. Eat your heart out, Leonardo.

By the age of fourteen Leibniz was ready to take on the University of Leipzig. Here he studied law, quickly expanding his studies to include all possible interpretations of this subject, including the laws of physics, the laws of philosophy, the laws of mathematics, and almost the entire political concept and history of law. It was during this period that Leibniz first came across the writings of such celebrated lawyers as Galileo, Descartes, and Hobbes, who were revolutionizing scientific, philosophical, and political thought. Characteristically, Leibniz soon conceived the idea of harmonizing all this radical thought with the Scholasticism that it was in the process of replacing. In his spare time Leibniz became an avid student of alchemy (with the aim of reconciling it to chemistry), and he also wrote a paper that set out the theoretical basis for a computer (almost three hundred years before Turing's seminal work on this subject).

By the time Leibniz had finished all this he was almost twenty, but when he applied for a degree the university told him he was too young. Having been found deficient in the one numerical system he was unable to master, Leibniz left Leipzig never to return. Instead he went to Altdorf, the university town of the free city of Nuremberg, where they immediately awarded him a doctor's degree and offered him a professorship. The latter he declined, saying that he had "very different things in mind."

Leibniz was ambitious and wanted to become a power to be reckoned with in the world. Fortunately for the world, he never achieved

14

this—at least not in the manner he hoped. (Yet what did he hope for? What, under the circumstances of the age, could he have hoped for? A leading political post? Are we to picture one of the greatest minds of all time working as chief advisory minister to a German princedom the size of Rhode Island? Goethe may have occupied a similar position a century later at Weimar, but this was all grist to the mill for literature. Leibniz would certainly have taken a more active role. We can only imagine what the new drainage scheme, the express carriages, the revolutionary windmills, the Harmonious Guild of Alchemists, and law courts presided over by calculating machines would have looked like with Leibniz in charge. To say nothing of the effect on the citizens' sanity.)

Doubtless with all this in mind, Leibniz now began putting himself about socially amongst the upper echelons of society. Eventually he was given a minor post at the court of the Prince elector, the Archbishop of Mainz, Johann Philip von Schönborn. The titles of German princes in those days were usually in inverse proportion to the size of the territory they ruled and their general importance. Johnny Beautifulborn's comparatively modest string of titles indicated a man with some clout on the German political scene.

At this time the map of German-speaking Europe looked like a Ming vase dropped from a great height and reassembled by a surrealist. This piece of rococo fantasy was called, with equally surrealist panache, the Holy Roman Empire (its name failed on all three counts). Most of the separate princedoms, palatinates, electorates, and whathaveyous which made up this unempire lived in a fairly easygoing, quasi-independent state, and the whole place was probably as oddly pleasant to live in as it looked on the map. Things were just beginning to pick up after the Thirty Years' War, and most people were only too pleased to live in a state of obscure provincialism ruled over by some harmless twit with an enormous name.

Unfortunately things were different across the Rhine in France—where instead of having nearly two hundred rulers and only one cheese worthy of the name, they now had just one ruler and a gastronomy fit for the Sun King at Versailles. Louis XIV was feeling in an expansive mood; France was Catholic, and many of the tiny German states across the Rhine were Protestant (or Catholic, it didn't really matter). The Archbishop of Mainz realized that somehow Louis had to be diverted from expanding into Germany. He discussed this matter with the bright young adviser who had just joined his staff, and in no time Leibniz proposed an ingenious scheme. Why didn't the archbishop try to interest Louis in a crusade, in mounting a great expedition to conquer Egypt? And if other countries could be persuaded to join in this holy war against the unbelievers, it might even pave the way to a harmonious reunion of the Catholic and Protestant churches.

The archbishop was overcome by this daring scheme, and Leibniz was at once dispatched to Paris to present it to Louis. But here Leibniz found himself encountering a few difficulties. It wasn't easy to gain an audience with the Sun King at Versailles. You had to persuade his ministers that you were on an important mission, and Louis's ministers didn't seem to appreciate the seriousness of Leibniz's plan. This included a wealth of compelling detail, including route maps, the size of army required, and diagrams of which cities to attack first. All these had been drawn up by a master German strategist whose purely theoretical military expertise and wide reading on the subject far outweighed that of any mere general. But Louis's ministers would insist on pointing out that France hadn't undertaken a crusade since the days of St. Louis, more than four centuries earlier.

Leibniz was to spend the next four years in Paris, though his enthusiasm for promoting his Egyptian project soon dwindled. He had far more important things to do (at the archbishop's expense). In those days Paris was recognized throughout Europe as the world's leading cultural and intellectual center, a situation which remains unchanged to this day in the eyes of its inhabitants. Leibniz quickly began circulating through the salons and attempting to meet as many leading intellectuals as he could. His temperament may have been that of a mad professor, but at this age he was still fairly good at disguising the fact. Fitted out in his best court finery, he cut quite an elegant figure, and under such circumstances his overpowering mental brilliance could easily be mistaken for sheer youthful vitality. The Duchess of Orleans, who appears to have regarded intellectuals much as we do now, was particularly impressed by this young German egghead: "It is so rare [for an intellectual] to be smartly dressed, and not to smell, and to understand jokes." The duchess, who on the side was a bit of an intellectual herself, soon befriended Leibniz—one of the earliest of a whole string of well-connected duchesses and princesses with whom Leibniz kept in contact for the rest of his life.

Despite all this socializing, Leibniz remained as mentally hyperactive as ever. A cornucopia of brilliant ideas flowed from his brain, several of such fundamental importance that any one of them would have guaranteed its originator immortality in his field. It was during this period that he invented integral and differential calculus. He also discovered binary arithmetic, though he assumed (wrongly) that the Chinese had discovered this before him—as he understood (correctly) that it was implicit in the Yin and Yang theories of the I Ching. (Such a perception is typical of Leibniz's sheer range.) Where the more familiar decimal system uses ten digits (0–9), binary arithmetic uses only two (0 and 1). This may appear long-winded, e.g., 1=1, 2=10, 3=11, 4=100, on to 9=1,001, 18=010010, and so forth. But Leibniz discovered that when certain categories of binary numbers (such as triples, for instance) are listed one below another, the 0s and 1s in the vertical columns often repeated in regular periods. This prompted him to hope that he might discover some entirely new general rules of mathematics—though he never realized this aim. He did realize, however, that binary is ideal for a mechanical system, which can work on simple stop-go or full-empty operations. With hindsight we can see that this is particularly the case for a system driven by electricity, with positive and negative. This has led to binary arithmetic being used in computers.

Leibniz attempted to exploit the mechanical advantage of binary, and even sketched a calculating machine which incorporated his new mathematics. Yet he soon realized that such a machine was beyond available technology.

At this time the new philosophy of Descartes (Cartesianism) was the structuralism of the day amongst the Parisian chattering classes. But unlike structuralism (which treats a text as a structure, devoid of an author) it could also be taken seriously. Descartes's philosophy represented a radical break with the Scholasticism of the medieval era. Instead of appealing to authority (that is, the largely Aristotelian teachings of the past), it was based upon reason and scientific method. Knowledge was built up, step by reasonable step, starting from indubitable certainty. The resemblance to mathematics was not coincidental. Descartes also excelled in this field. It was he who proposed the notion of coordinate geometry (whose Cartesian coordinates are named after him). By means of three axes (coordinates) standing at right angles to one another in three dimensions, the position of any point in space could be plotted with coordinate values.

Not surprisingly, this combination of mathematics, reason, and scientific method led Descartes to adopt a mechanistic view of the world. The universe was like a huge machine or clock mechanism which had initially been set in motion by God. Likewise, objects existed in absolute space: there was an absolute difference between their positions, and they were either absolutely at rest, or in motion.

Leibniz ingeniously perceived a flaw in this argument. According to this absolutist view, space must be different from the objects that are at rest, or in motion, within it. In which case space must be completely uniform throughout, like an absolute emptiness. But if so, how can we use it to measure location by means of coordinates? Such coordinates must inevitably be imaginary—they couldn't actually exist in this featureless uniformity. But if such coordinates are imaginary, they must be arbitrarily imposed on space by us. So how can we possibly know that they are stationary? What would they be stationary in reference to?

Here we can see in embryo the argument for Einstein's relativity. But instead of investigating this in mathematical terms (like Einstein), Leibniz chose to see it in terms of metaphysics. Here lay the germ of Leibniz's mature philosophy.

In light of his preceding argument, Leibniz came to the remarkable conclusion that space did not exist. (He used a similar argument concerning time, coming to the same conclusion.) Leibniz maintained that as there was no absolute frame of reference, our notions of space and time were mere superstitious assumptions. When examined in the light of his argument, only things existed. The idea that one thing was faster than another, appeared at a later time than another, or was closer to us than another, depended entirely upon our relativistic point of view. Another person, viewing from another perspective, would see things differently. There was no absolute space or time: they simply didn't exist. Only God was able to see things as they really were—from an utterly perspectiveless viewpoint devoid of space and time. So far Leibniz's philosophy has distinct echoes of Platonic idealism—where the particular world around us is seen as an illusion reflecting an ultimate reality of ideal forms. But the new Cartesianism had shown how it was possible to base philosophic truth upon reason rather than on an unseen transcendent reality of ideas. Although Leibniz didn't entirely agree with Descartes, he felt there was no going back to such an unscientific idealistic approach as Plato's. Instead of Descartes's mechanistic view of the world, Leibniz proposed a dynamic picture involving kinetic energy. As a result of Leibniz's discovery of calculus, whose calculations involved diminishing values receding to the infinitesimally small, he came to see that things ultimately consisted of infinitesimally small points which had neither space nor time as attributes. These he would eventually call "monads."

During his time in Paris, in the early 1670s, Leibniz also conceived of another important notion, which was to play a major role in his later mature philosophy. This was the principle of sufficient reason, which maintains that nothing occurs without there being a sufficient reason for it to do so. Leibniz's principle was to become one of the main tenets of rationalist philosophy.

But first it is necessary to place this principle within the context of Leibniz's other evolving ideas. One of his central ideas was his *scientia generalis,* his own version of a scientific method. This emphasized rational analysis and reduction. It involved the analysis of concepts into their simplest elements. (The word *analysis* comes from the Greek word "to unravel.") These simplest elements are expressed as definitions. The strictly logical analysis of concepts reduces them to logically necessary truths—that is, truths which must be the case—as in any definition. But these definitions can be combined to form truths that are synthetic—that is, truths which do not follow of logical necessity.

For Leibniz there were thus three types of truth. First, there were truths that could be reduced to definition. For example: Euclid's definition, "An acute angle is an angle less than a right angle." Second, there were identical propositions, such as one finds in mathematics. For instance: 142,857 x 7 = 999,999. All truths derived from reason can be reduced to one or the other of these two types of truth. The third type of truth consisted of empirical propositions—those which could be derived from experience. For example: "The River Thames runs through London." This is not a logically necessary truth, it is contingent.

But a perceptive contemporary critic of Leibniz pointed out that not all truths fall into these three categories. This is noticeably the case in the axioms of mathematics. Take, for instance, Euclid's axioms: "The whole is greater than the part" and "Things which are equal to the same thing are also equal to one another" (in other words, if A = B, and B = C, it follows that A = C). These statements may seem evident enough, but strictly speaking neither of these axioms is either a definition or an identical proposition. They somehow just manage to fall between the two. Leibniz was willing to concede this, but he maintained that such axioms had to be accepted if science was to move forward in any way. He also suggested a method of validating such axioms by means of the principle of contradiction. He maintained that such truths were in fact logically necessary because to maintain their opposite would lead to a contradiction.

The principle of contradiction laid the foundation for mathematics as well as for all that is logically possible. But just because something is logically possible doesn't mean that it actually happens. In order to account rationally for what actually exists, a second principle was required. Instead of simply avoiding contradiction, science required a sufficient reason for something to take place. This principle of sufficient reason stated that nothing happened in the world without there being a sufficient reason why it should happen in this way and no other. But here again Leibniz departed from science and entered the realms of metaphysics. He would use the principle of sufficient reason to demonstrate the existence of God as well as many other metaphysical and theological features that concurred with the Christianity of his day.

Yet apart from these far-reaching theoretical

ideas, Leibniz had not lost his touch in less reasonable matters. He drew up plans for a hand-operated boat which could travel beneath the surface of the water; a compressed air engine whose explosive side effects could be used for firing projectiles; and he even considered the possibility of a ship that could travel through space—though the latter was abandoned when he correctly surmised that there wouldn't be enough air to power the mechanical sails.

Then, suddenly, the bottom fell out of Leibniz's world. In 1673 the Archbishop of Mainz died. Leibniz's wages were stopped, and the attempt to interest Louis XIV in an Egyptian crusade was abandoned. (Speculation has arisen that Napoleon may have been influenced by this plan when he undertook his remarkably similar expedition to Egypt more than a century later. It's now known that Napoleon did in fact see Leibniz's plans when he occupied Hanover in 1803 and Leibniz's papers were discovered in the archives—but this was four years after his disastrous campaign to the Nile. If Napoleon had seen Leibniz's plans a few years previously, might they have enabled him to defeat Nelson at the Battle of the Nile? We know what Leibniz would have thought.)

Leibniz now found himself confronted with a practical problem which has defeated many of the finest intellectual minds in history. How on earth was he to earn a living? At once he began sending out letters of recommendation to courts throughout Germany: did they wish to take up this unique opportunity to employ a genius in residence? Meanwhile, to bring in some ready cash he set about making a revolutionary calculating machine, which overcame the difficulties of Pascal's earlier version. Unfortunately Leibniz was diverted from his far-reaching theoretical speculations on this matter. His prime need was to try to make his machine commercially viable as quickly as possible, otherwise he might have come up with the first computer almost 150 years before Babbage (who was himself almost 150 years ahead of his time). This is no far-fetched claim on Leibniz's behalf. As we have seen, he had already invented a binary mathematics, an element that would become crucial in the development of mechanical computation. He had also written a paper which outlined the combinatorial mathematics that were to play such an essential role in computer theory. This is the branch of mathematics that analyzes the possible outcomes of a given situation, or problem, by breaking it down into simple, discrete elements. The resemblance between the workings of a computer and Leibniz's analysis of scientific method, his *scientia generalis*, now becomes evident. And, as we shall see, although Leibniz's conception of nature was not strictly mechanical, its deterministic workings would bear many resemblances to those of a computer.

Leibniz remained in Paris until 1676, when he was finally offered a position by Johann Friedrich, Duke of Braunschweig-Lüneburg, Zelle, and Hanover. Reluctantly Leibniz was forced to set out for Hanover—though he contrived to travel by a somewhat roundabout route, via London and then The Hague, where he filched a number of useful ideas from Spinoza. Leibniz was to remain in the employ of the Hanover court for the rest of his life. His first post was as librarian, and with his usual verve he immediately set about trying to do almost everything else except run the library. He was determined to assist his master in every possible way with the ruling of his duchy. The duke was presented with a continuous stream of new ideas and schemes: a novel monetary policy, a proposal for the utilization of unused warmth in chimneys, a blueprint for linking all the river systems in the duchy by a network of canals, a newly invented fountain for the palace gardens, a national insurance scheme (more than two hundred years ahead of its time), and a number of suggestions for further positions that Leibniz could usefully occupy—head of a tribunal to overhaul the duchy's educational system, inspector of waters, of transport, of cloisters, etc. (all salaries to be paid concurrently, one assumes). Leibniz wasn't a greedy man, but once he set his mind to something—such as earning money, or reorganizing the palace drainage system—it would always produce a flood of new ideas.

It wasn't long before the duke found his patience tried to the limit. The court had had enough. How on earth were they going to get rid of this new librarian? Eventually it was decided to send him off to the Harz Mountains, to see if he could devise a new pumping system to prevent the duchy's mines from flooding. An odd job for a librarian, but then this was certainly an odd librarian.

Around this time Leibniz began to revive his interest in alchemy. It may seem curious that a mind of Leibniz's caliber and rationalistic bent should have been attracted to such a spurious subject as alchemy. But in fact alchemy wasn't quite so spurious in those days. Experimental chemistry had not yet come of age as a separate science, and many of its practices still remained largely within the realms of alchemy, which had nurtured these techniques through many centuries of esoteric practice. In the seventeenth century, chemists and alchemists were often indistinguishable. (Only now that alchemists are extinct is it so easy to tell them apart.)

But none of this excuses Leibniz, who was interested in alchemy for the most gullible of reasons. If he could discover the philosopher's stone, if only a way could be found to transmute base metals into gold, he could become financially independent. Then he wouldn't have to spend so much of his valuable time avoiding his official duties in the court library. Throughout his years at Hanover, Leibniz was constantly having itinerant alchemists summoned to the court so they could demonstrate to him their powers. He was so impressed with one Jonathan Crafft that he went into business with him, financing his experiments. This was a major departure for Leibniz, who was notoriously cheap. Whenever anyone was married at court, and protocol required that he should give them a wedding present, he would present the couple with a homemade booklet containing his own philosophical maxims regarding married life.

In 1680 the old Duke of Hanover died "at the age of 64 years, 2 months, 2 days and 3 hours," as Leibniz noted in his correspondence. The duke was succeeded by his brother, who was keen on securing for himself the added title "Elector of Hanover." In order to further his case he decided to put his librarian to work in the archives, researching his genealogy and at the same time writing a family history. Leibniz retired to the library and emerged some time later with a revolutionary treatise setting out his ideas on calculus. The reaction to this document at court is not recorded, but when it was published in Europe it caused a furor. Newton claimed that he had discovered calculus long ago, and that Leibniz had stolen the idea from his unpublished papers which he had been shown in London. In no time a great controversy was raging, and the finest minds in Europe began taking sides, writing angry letters to the learned journals.

In fact Newton *had* discovered calculus first; but Leibniz had discovered it independently, some time before he had seen Newton's unpublished papers. Leibniz was involved in several controversies about plagiarism during his life. He was so brilliant that he had no need to be a plagiarist, and he was temperamentally averse to incorporating ideas put forward by others into his own work. But there were times when he saw radical implications in the ideas of others, which appeared to remain unrealized by their authors. He would then sometimes consider the original idea as his own property because he had made better use of it. This was certainly the case when he pillaged some of Spinoza's ideas.

The political situation in Europe remained dangerous. The loose federation of German states, the so-called Holy Roman Empire, was under threat from all sides. Louis XIV had taken Strasbourg and was laying claim to much of Alsace; there had been a Hungarian revolt in the east; and the Turks were at the gates of Vienna. Despite all of Leibniz's harebrained schemes, he remained a persuasive student of practical statecraft. From his base at the court in Hanover he continued to correspond with his widening circle of royal and aristocratic admirers, putting forward a number of highly perceptive political proposals. These contained not only a variety of ad hoc solutions to the problems of the day but also a number of more farsighted schemes. One of Leibniz's prevailing pet ideas was to engineer the reunification of the Catholic and Protestant churches. This he hoped would lead eventually to a united Europe. Over the years he attempted in vain to interest Peter the Great, Louis XIV, and the Holy Roman Emperor in this scheme—all to no avail.

But the Duke of Hanover still wanted to become the Elector of Hanover, and began wondering what Leibniz was doing about this highly important project—which was, after all, what he was being paid for. Eventually, as a result of Leibniz's rather begrudging and belated researches, the duke was promoted to Elector of Hanover. Amidst the ensuing celebrations, Leibniz's somewhat tardy delivery was tactfully overlooked. Then in 1798 the Elector died, and was replaced by George Ludwig.

Unlike his predecessor, Ludwig was a lowbrow roisterer who wasn't in the least interested in the latest intellectual ideas of his librarian. Leibniz was summoned to explain why he had not yet produced the Hanover family history that he had been ordered to write—a work provisionally entitled "The History of the House of Braunschweig-Lüneburg, and Hanover, Including the Celle and Wolfenbüttel Branches, Relating also to the House of Guelf and the Este Family, Starting from Earliest Times." This title was almost certainly longer than any final text of the book which had yet been written, and Leibniz was ordered back to the library with a flea in his ear. Reluctantly he set to work researching, but he quickly became diverted by an ambitious scheme to set out in detail his entire philosophy.

Leibniz's philosophy is a system of great beauty and in its essentials, surprising simplicity. He held that there are an infinite number of substances that make up the world. These are called monads, and are the ultimate constituents of all things, including God. If something occupies space it must have extension; this means it can be divided and is thus complex. Therefore these ultimate simple monads cannot have extension and are consequently not material. So the world is made up of an infinite number of metaphysical points. But as these points are metaphysical, they can have no physical interaction. They are not subject to the laws of cause and effect: there is no causality between them, despite what appears to us to happen in the material world. The apparent interaction of the monads that make up the world is the result of a "pre-established harmony" that exists between them, and has existed since their substance was first created by God. From then on, the changes in the state of each individual monad were caused by the preceding state of that monad. In other words, they are each subject to their own chain of causality, which remains in alignment with all other monads because of their "pre-established harmony." This was created by God, and all nature is the clock of God ("horlogium dei"). What exists may not be a perfect creation, but its imperfection is unavoidable owing to its nature.

Leibniz was able to prove this by means of his two fundamental principles—that of contradiction, and that of sufficient reason. God may have been infinite, but when it came to creating the world his infinite possibilities were limited. Why? In order to create this world, it had of necessity to be a possible world. And for it to be possible, it had to conform to the principle of contradiction (or it would not have been possible). Likewise, for the world to be created at all there had to be a sufficient reason. This was God. Because God was good, he would of course create the best world. But according to the principle of contradiction, this had to be a possible world. This meant that God had created "the best of all possible worlds." A perfect world was evidently impossible, and whatever defects the world had were inevitable owing to its possibleness.

It was this aspect of Leibniz's philosophy that led Voltaire to satirize him in *Candide* as Dr. Pangloss. The ridiculous Dr. Pangloss airily persists in proclaiming that "All is for the best in this the best of all possible worlds"—regardless of the world's evils and such catastrophes as the Lisbon earthquake which killed thirty thousand people. Similarly, it was this part of Leibniz's philosophy that Bertrand Russell, the Voltaire of the early twentieth century, was to describe as a shallow optimistic metaphysics for princesses. Russell extended this criticism to Leibniz's entire Monadology, the name of the book that Leibniz eventually published in 1714 to explain his philosophy of monads. Despite this, Leibniz's *Monadology* is a work of considerable ingenuity and complexity.

In this final version of his ever-developing ideas he explains how each of the infinite number of monads existing in pre-established harmony is utterly individual. Leibniz envisaged these monads as being like souls: they are metaphysical, immortal, and each one is unique. Each monad is "windowless" in that it has no perception or effect on the monads around it; yet at the same time each monad is said to mirror the universe. Together they exist in an exhaustive hierarchy. Superior monads have a higher degree of consciousness: they mirror the universe much more clearly and distinctly. Others are dimmer in this aspect. Yet no two monads have precisely the same amount of consciousness or it would be impossible to tell them apart—and thus they would not be uniquely individual. The human body, for instance, consists of a myriad of monads, the most superior of which is its soul—which is possessed of the highest consciousness.

But why should every monad be unique? Why couldn't there be two monads that are the same? Leibniz is quite explicit on this point, and even evokes a principle to back up his assertion. This is his "identity of indiscernibles," according to which there couldn't be two things that were utterly the same because they would then be one and the very same thing. They would be completely indiscernible and thus identical! Leibniz even makes ingenious use of the Principle of Sufficient Reason to "prove" his point. Suppose God had placed two indiscernibles—the first one here, the second one there. There would be no sufficient reason why he should not have placed them the other way about. Thus the Principle of Sufficient Reason, which was necessary for the world to exist, would have been violated. At the higher realms of rationality, even reason can begin to appear irrational.

Leibniz was not afraid to grasp the often curious implications of his rigid rationalistic approach. The idea that each monad contained its own more or less clear consciousness of the entire universe, together with his previously mentioned proof that time did not exist, led him to an intriguing conclusion. Each monad must contain within it a consciousness of its entire life in the universe. But since the soul of each human being is a monad, he concluded "that the individual notion of each person involves once and for all everything that will ever happen to him." This may find faint echoes in some modern psychological theory, but it directly contravened the Christianity of the period. Such an idea would have rendered Judgment Day not only irrelevant but unjust. Here was another theory that Leibniz prudently consigned to his drawer.

All this monadology may sound to us, as it did to Bertrand Russell, like an overly ingenious fairy tale. It also has a number of apparent flaws. How, for instance, can the material world consist of immaterial objects? Leibniz explains that this is merely their "appearance." Such intellectual sleight of hand remains unsatisfactory to the modern sensibility, which is more attuned to the hard facts of scientific explanation. Yet Leibniz's monads bear a striking—if inadvertent—resemblance to certain elements at the cutting edge of modern scientific thinking. The material nucleus of an atom is the size of a pea in a cathedral compared to the size of the atom that contains it. Not much material here. In other words, our so-called material world consists of an awful lot of "immateriality." Also, quantum theory often treats the electrons that orbit the atomic nucleus as mere waves, without material substance. Likewise, even the contents of the atomic nucleus have now been analyzed into entities that often tend to bear more resemblance to energy than matter. Leibniz was of course not arguing on the scientific level, the physical level. His monads were indisputably metaphysical. What is interesting is that his purely rational philosophizing should bear such an uncanny resemblance to modern scientific materialistic theorizing. How much do we really know about the world? And how much of what we do know is dictated by our way of thinking? Leibniz concluded that we do not perceive the ultimate constituents of the universe. All we perceive is their appearance. Plato placed this ultimate reality in a transcendent world of ideas. Leibniz's monads may be metaphysical and extensionless, but they are undeniably in this world. They are of it; indeed, they are what our world consists of.

Here Leibniz was broaching one of the most profound questions that continues to beset human knowledge, both scientific and philosophical. Our knowledge of the world depends entirely upon our perceptual apparatus: sight, touch, smell, hearing, and so forth. Especially sight. We tend to convince ourselves that the real world is as we see it. Yet even here, at our most accomplished perception, we have in the last century or so discovered that there are aspects of this world that we are incapable of "seeing." At both ends of the visible spectrum we know that things exist beyond the limits of our ability to perceive them. There is ultraviolet and infrared, to say nothing of radio waves, cosmic rays, and so forth. These we can measure only with scientific instruments. Yet these subtle scientific instruments have, in a very purposive sense, been developed only as extensions of our perceptual apparatus. They are not categorically different from our sight, touch, and other senses. Yet how do we know that the ultimate reality "out there" matches our perceptual apparatus, or even our highly sophisticated scientific extensions of it? The fact is, we don't. And it would seem that we simply have no way of knowing whether it does or not. All we perceive is the appearance that our perceptual apparatus is capable of perceiving. What resemblance can this possibly have to the ultimate reality that stimulates our perception? In a very real sense, any answer to this question would seem to be inconceivable. Leibniz's rationalistic philosophy was the first modern attempt to answer this question in terms of an overall explanation of the world. His "system" would in time inspire the great philosophic system-builders. But first philosophy would have to pay much closer attention to the scientific revolution that was already well under way during Leibniz's lifetime. The system of Leibniz's monadology was in its own way a philosophical answer to the great all-embracing scientific system that Newton had established less than three decades earlier with gravity.

Leibniz's other major contribution was in the

field of logic. This was to prove the first major advance in logic since Aristotle. Unfortunately Leibniz had a great admiration for Aristotle, recognizing in him one of the very few polymaths in history superior to himself. Leibniz accepted that much of the medieval Scholasticism derived from Aristotle was (after two millennia) now redundant. But he seems to have regarded Aristotle's logic as sacrosanct. Whenever his conclusions differed fundamentally from those of Aristotle, he couldn't help feeling that somewhere there must have been a hidden flaw in his reasoning, some intricate point he had overlooked. Others, more plausibly, see this as nonsense. They maintain that in fact he was afraid of becoming embroiled in public controversy. Aristotle's logic was still the official teaching of the church. To deny this might well have finished off his diplomatic career as well as disrupting his social and intellectual contacts with princesses and rulers throughout Europe.

Either way, Leibniz chose to consign his own logic to the oblivion of his voluminous trunk, where it would remain undiscovered for a century and a half. By this time some (but by no means all) of his logical innovations had been discovered by others.

Leibniz's logic is a product of his supreme belief in rationalism. It also harks back to his *scientia generalis,* providing its underpinning. As in the *scientia,* Leibniz believed that most general concepts are "composite." That is, they are made up of a determinable number of fundamental basic concepts. He believed that it was possible to represent these "iconically," with signs or symbols indicating their content. This could be done in the manner of Chinese or ancient Egyptian hieroglyphs. In this way it would be possible to create a "universal characteristic language." This would not only be understood by all, it would also convey the basic concepts common to all humanity. It would be an international language of ideas, comparable in its exactitude to the universal language of numbers. And where numbers could be used in the calculations of mathematics, the Leibniz hieroglyphs could be used in a "calculus of reason." Leibniz foresaw a future for this method which would transform many of our social habits from their current messy inexactitude into incontrovertible rationalist practice. "If controversies were to arise, there would be no more need of disputation between two philosophers than between two accountants. For it would suffice to take their pencils in their hands, to sit down to their slates, and to say to each other (with a friend as witness, if they liked): 'Let us calculate.'" All court cases, social controversies, all manner of disputes would be settled with the efficiency and finality of a mathematical sum. Indeed, the answers could even be checked by calculating machines, to show there had been no mistakes. And by reversing the process it would also be possible to check—rationally—whether any composite concept rested on a solid foundation of basic concepts. Or whether it in fact inadvertently included some faulty supposition.

These processes would all involve Leibniz's "universally characteristic language." This is now generally recognized as the first symbolic logic (though it was not the origin of modern symbolic logic, because it remained hidden for

150 years in Leibniz's trunk). Unfortunately Leibniz was not able to overcome the difficulties that would plague its later independent discoverers. Symbolic logic operates in much the same manner as algebra, with general symbols. "All apples are fruit" can be reduced to "All As are Bs," which becomes in Leibniz's symbolic notation "A ∞ B." Such algebra was unable to deal satisfactorily with particular statements as well as negative ones. But the sheer importance of symbolic logic cannot be overemphasized. Two centuries after Leibniz's initial foundation, this subject would be playing the major role in both philosophy and the foundations of mathematics. At the turn of the twentieth century Bertrand Russell himself would take part in a major attempt to place mathematics on a sound logical footing. (A vain endeavor, as it transpired.) Meanwhile much philosophical energy was being expounded (and continues to be expounded) on the logical analysis of language. A major part of this consists of the unraveling of composite concepts into their constituent parts, just as Leibniz prescribed. Leibniz's misguided

attempt to reduce the richness of social intercourse to a logical formula remains with us to this day.

In 1700 William Duke of Gloucester, heir to the throne of England, died. This raised the distinct possibility that George Ludwig of Hanover would become the heir. Negotiations opened between London and Hanover, and George Ludwig decided to make use of his librarian's political and genealogical expertise, which was so highly esteemed throughout the courts of Europe. The negotiations with London eventually ended in success, and George Ludwig was established as the heir to the throne of England. Leibniz claimed he was largely responsible for this, but subsequent researches have revealed a different picture. It appears that Leibniz very nearly wrecked these delicate negotiations when it was discovered he had entered into secret negotiations of his own with the help of a Scottish spy called Ker of Kersland.

Leibniz now spent an increasing amount of time visiting nearby courts, where he managed to secure for himself a number of appointments (all full time, on full pay). For several years he had already been chief librarian of the famous collection at Wolfenbüttel, though he was specifically forbidden from implementing any of his schemes for reorganizing the collection, despite his repeated suggestions. Also, as a result of his correspondence with the Electress Sophie Charlotte (the future queen of Prussia), the German Academy of Sciences was founded in Berlin. Leibniz naturally made sure that he was appointed as its first president, even if the pay did somewhat disappoint him. In 1711 he met Peter the Great of Russia, who was so impressed by the philosopher that he appointed him a counselor to the Russian court. Yet despite his many posts Leibniz continued to devote himself almost exclusively to matters unrelated to his official duties. This is fortunate, for his work in the fields of mathematics and logic dating from this period seem to have been of more lasting value than discovering a new method for dredging the palace ponds.

In 1712 Leibniz set out from Hanover for Vienna. Here he began by presenting a few of his ideas to the emperor. Included among these was the proposal that his imperial majesty should resign, disband his thousand-year-old empire, and amalgamate it with Russia and France. To the surprise of no one, except Leibniz, the emperor chose to ignore this proposal—and also surprised Leibniz by ignoring his request for a high-ranking post in the imperial administration. By this stage Leibniz was in the employ of no less than five different courts, though to give him his due he always considered that Hanover had first call on his services (if we may call them such). Hanover too remained under this impression, and astonishingly continued to pay their absentee librarian his wages. Leibniz had now been working on the History of Braunschweig-Lüneburg, etc. for more than thirty years. During this extended period his chronicle appears to have reached as far as the Dark Ages. But George Ludwig, the future king of England, wasn't impressed when he learned that the family history still had over a thousand years to cover before his arrival on the scene. In fact, as

one commentator has pointed out, all the Han-
overians probably wanted right from the start
was a small booklet which they could hand
around to impress their fellow rulers. Threaten-
ing letters began arriving in Vienna from Hanover, demanding Leibniz's return. In the end the
Hanoverian authorities even took the drastic
step of cutting off his salary. But Leibniz was far
too busy petitioning for posts, attempting to set
up a Society of Sciences (guess who would be
president), making proposals for the future of
Europe, doing linguistic research, making mag-
netic observations in Siberia, etc. After two
years, when Leibniz heard that Queen Anne of
England had died, he immediately hurried back
across Europe to Hanover, ready to accompany
his master to England—where the new royal administration would doubtless have innumerable
posts at its disposal.

Leibniz arrived in Hanover to discover that
George Ludwig had departed for England three
days earlier. But his chief employer had not for-
gotten his absentee librarian and had left specific
instructions concerning his employment. From

now on Leibniz was not to be allowed to leave Hanover. It seems he was placed under virtual palace arrest. Poor Leibniz. Anyone of interest or influence had been removed to England, and all that remained in Hanover were the bitter dregs of the court. They despised Leibniz, and he now became an object of ridicule. The fashionable young philosopher who had once graced the salons of Paris and Vienna was now approaching seventy. He walked with a stoop which made him look like a hunchback, but still insisted upon wearing stylish clothes. Unfortunately, owing to Leibniz's stinginess, these long-serving clothes were now in the style of a bygone era. Elaborate ruffs and tall black wigs had long since passed out of fashion; as one courtier put it, Leibniz looked like "an archaeological find."

The coronation of George I duly took place in London; and Leibniz, ever the optimist, began sending a few initial proposals regarding posts he felt himself best equipped to occupy. Despite his record on the family history, Leibniz in all seriousness suggested that he be appointed historian of England. Still no summons came from the royal court. Leibniz felt deeply humiliated. But he continued working as ever, producing further additions to his trunkloads of papers. He even brought The History of Braunschweig-Lüneburg, etc. as far as the year 1009. Then, in the autumn of 1716, he began suffering from severe gout and was forced to retire to his bed for lengthy periods. He soon grew increasingly frail, and finally on November 14, 1716, Leibniz died. Although George I was on a visit to a nearby palace at the time, neither he nor any of the court came to Leibniz's funeral. This was attended solely by his faithful secretary Eckhart, who was to write the first memoir of his unique employer. The picture he paints is of an often distracted, rather strange man, who spoke ill of no one. Apparently his only known pleasure was inviting the palace children to play on the carpet in his room. As they left he would present them each with a little cake, and then return to his papers, at which he sometimes worked for days and nights on end without rising from his chair.

Afterword

Leibniz was the first of the great German philosophers. He was also the first of his countrymen to produce an all-embracing philosophical system—which was to become something of a forte in German philosophy. The tradition that began with Leibniz would pass down through a roll call which contains the majority of outstanding philosophical figures during the last two hundred years. This line includes Kant, Hegel, Schopenhauer, Nietzsche, Wittgenstein, and Heidegger.

During this period a similar process was taking place in music, which the Germans also came to regard very much as their domain. This time the roll call extends from Bach, through Mozart and Beethoven, to Wagner. Many reasons have been suggested for this domination. One of the more plausible has to do with the shared nature of philosophy and music. Neither involves articulate expression concerning the business of everyday life, such as is found in the novel.

These were the years of growing Prussian domination over the fragmented German states. Freedom of expression was considered highly undesirable by the authorities and the all-pervasive bureaucracy. Many intelligent and creative figures who might otherwise have written novels chose instead to become musicians or philosophers. For the most part such people dealt with "higher things." No articulate challenge was posed to the bureaucratic status quo. Even so, Kant was to have his works banned for a period during the reign of Frederick the Great. Yet by the time we come to his successor Hegel, we find his systematic philosophy glorifying the similarly systematic state. Admittedly this system was castigated by Hegel's contemporary Schopenhauer. But Schopenhauer only challenged

Hegel's philosophical system, not the state system. He remained extremely conservative in his political views, and his pessimistic philosophy was almost totally ignored until the last years of his life.

Much the same fate befell the other great nineteenth-century nonconformist German philosopher. Later in the century, Nietzsche too would remain almost completely ignored during his lifetime, and would also spend most of his time in exile. Only when he fell victim to madness did he return to Germany, where he was institutionalized for the last decade of his life.

Such attitudes in Germany toward its philosophers were to be echoed in the twentieth century. By contrast to his predecessors, Wittgenstein was a sophisticated Viennese Jew (indicatively, from the same city and of the same religion as his contemporary Freud). Wittgenstein too spent most of his life in exile, teaching at Cambridge in England. Meanwhile the other great figure of German philosophy, Heidegger, remained teaching philosophy at Freiburg. Like Hegel, he chose to support the state, though by now the rigid authoritarianism of Prussian domination had given way to the racist fantasies of Hitler's dictatorship. It is difficult to imagine a serious philosopher identifying with such rubbish, but in Heidegger's case this appears to have happened largely through weakness of character and careerist ambition. Heidegger's philosophy itself is open to a wide variety of interpretations. These range from the existentialism of Sartre to the structuralism of Derrida and Foucault (including, it must be added, certain "folkish" elements of fascism). At any rate, with Heidegger one branch of the great German tradition begun by Leibniz seems to have come to an end. Its offshoots have now taken root elsewhere in Europe, where they have acquired a weird and wonderful structuralist bloom with an unmistakably French perfume.

The other branch of the German tradition in philosophy, represented by Wittgenstein, has petered out into a wilderness of linguistic analysis. For the followers of Wittgenstein, the great questions of philosophy are reduced to little more than linguistic errors. Leibniz may have made many errors in his life, and indeed in his philosophy, but fortunately these were much more interesting than mere linguistic ones.

From Leibniz's Writings

The monad, of which we shall speak here, is nothing but a simple substance which enters into compounds; simple, that is to say, without parts.

There must be simple substances, because there are compounds; for the compound is nothing but a collection or aggregate of simples.

Where there are no parts, neither extension, shape, nor divisibility is possible. And these monads are the true atoms of nature. In a word, they are the elements of things.

—*Monadology,* Sections 1–3

There is no fear of a monad dissolving, and there

is no possible way in which such a simple substance could perish in the course of nature.

For the same reason there is no way in which a simple substance could begin in the course of nature, since it cannot be made out of any compounds.

In this way it can be said that monads can only begin and end all at once. That is to say, they can only begin by creation and end by annihilation, whereas what is compound begins or ends in parts.

—*Monadology*, Sections 4–6

There is no way of explaining how a monad can be altered or changed within itself by any other created thing, since it is impossible to move anything in it or to conceive of the possibility of any internal motion being started. Such a motion could neither be started, given direction, increased, nor decreased within it, as can take place in compounds, where change among the parts can take place. Monads have no windows by which anything could come in or go out.

—*Monadology*, Section 7

Primitive truths, which are known by means of intuition, are of two kinds. They are either truths of reason, or truths of fact. Truths of reason are necessary. That is to say, they cannot be denied: their opposite is impossible. Truths of fact are contingent. That is to say, their opposite is possible. Primitive truths of reason are those which I call by the general name of "identicals," because it seems they only repeat the same thing in a different manner, without teaching us anything. Those which are affirmative are such as the following: "Everything is what is," "A is A, B is B," "The equilateral rectangle is a rectangle." . . . Now we come to the negative identicals, which depend either upon the principle of contradiction or upon that of disparates. The principle of contradiction is in general: A proposition is either true or false . . .

—*Collected Writings,* Volume V, 343

Our reasoning is founded on two great principles: the principle of contradiction, or, what comes to the same thing, that of identity. . . . Secondly there is the principle of sufficient reason, by virtue of which we consider that no fact can be real or existing, and no proposition can be true unless there is a sufficient reason why it should be thus and not otherwise, even though in most cases these reasons cannot be known to us.

—*Monadology*, early sections

Regarding the proposition that three is equal to two plus one—this is only the definition of the term three. It is true that this contains a hidden proposition: namely, that the ideas of these numbers are possible. Here this is known intuitively, thus we can say that intuitive knowledge is contained in definitions when their possibility is immediately evident.

—*Monadology*, opening sections

It is perfectly correct to say there is an infinite of things. That is, there are always more things than one can specify. But it is easy to demonstrate that there is no infinite number, infinite line, or any other infinite quantity, if these are taken as genuine wholes. . . . Strictly speaking, the true infinite exists only in the absolute, which precedes all composition and is not formed by the addition of parts. . . . The thought of finite and infinite is only appropriate wherever there is a magnitude or multiplicity. The genuine infinite is not a "modification": it is the absolute. Indeed, it is precisely by modifying it that one limits oneself and forms the finite.

—*New Essays on Human Understanding,*
Chapter 17

Each monad (or substance) has something of the infinite, in that it involves its cause: God. That is to say, it has some trace of omniscience and omnipotence. For in the perfect notion of each individual substance there are contained all its predicates, both necessary and contingent, as well as its past, present, and future. Each monad (or substance) expresses the whole universe according to its situation and aspect, in so far as things are referred to it. Thus it is necessary that some of our perceptions, be they ever so clear, remain confused, since they involve things which are infinite.

—*Collected Writings*, Volume II, 311

The notion of pre-established harmony results from the notion of monads (or substance). For according to this, the idea of each monad (or substance) involves all that will ever happen to it. . . . True, there is a miracle involved in the system of pre-established harmony. But this is only in the beginning, where God enters into it. After this everything goes its own way in the phenomena of nature, according to the laws of souls and bodies. . . . This hypothesis is not gratuitous, even though it cannot be proved a priori.

—*Collected Writings*, Volume III, 144

My philosophy . . . is not complete in itself, and I do not claim to have a reason for everything which other people have thought they could explain. . . . It is my view that the majority of philosophical systems are for the most part correct in what they claim to be true, but not so much in what they claim to be untrue.

—*Collected Writings,* Letters

The good is divided into the virtuous, the pleasing, and the useful. However, I believe that essentially something must be either pleasing in itself, or conducive to something else which can give us a pleasant feeling. That is to say, the good is either pleasing or useful. Virtue itself consists in a pleasure of the mind.

—*New Essays on Human Understanding,*
Chapter 20

Chronology of Significant Philosophical Dates

6th C B.C.	The beginning of Western philosophy with Thales of Miletus.
End of 6th C B.C.	Death of Pythagoras.
399 B.C.	Socrates sentenced to death in Athens.
c 387 B.C.	Plato founds the Academy in Athens, the first university.
335 B.C.	Aristotle founds the Lyceum in Athens, a rival school to the Academy.

324 A.D.	Emperor Constantine moves capital of Roman Empire to Byzantium.
400 A.D.	St. Augustine writes his *Confessions*. Philosophy absorbed into Christian theology.
410 A.D.	Sack of Rome by Visigoths heralds opening of Dark Ages.
529 A.D.	Closure of Academy in Athens by Emperor Justinian marks end of Hellenic thought.
Mid-13th C	Thomas Aquinas writes his commentaries on Aristotle. Era of Scholasticism.
1453	Fall of Byzantium to Turks, end of Byzantine Empire.
1492	Columbus reaches America. Renaissance in Florence and revival of interest in Greek learning.
1543	Copernicus publishes *On the Revolution of the Celestial Orbs*, proving mathematically that the earth revolves around the sun.

1633	Galileo forced by church to recant heliocentric theory of the universe.
1641	Descartes publishes his *Meditations*, the start of modern philosophy.
1677	Death of Spinoza allows publication of his *Ethics*.
1687	Newton publishes *Principia*, introducing concept of gravity.
1689	Locke publishes *Essay Concerning Human Understanding*. Start of empiricism.
1710	Berkeley publishes *Principles of Human Knowledge*, advancing empiricism to new extremes.
1716	Death of Leibniz.
1739–1740	Hume publishes *Treatise of Human Nature*, taking empiricism to its logical limits.
1781	Kant, awakened from his "dogmatic slumbers" by Hume, publishes *Critique of Pure Reason*.

Great era of German metaphysics begins.

1807   Hegel publishes *The Phenomenology of Mind*, high point of German metaphysics.

1818   Schopenhauer publishes *The World as Will and Representation*, introducing Indian philosophy into German metaphysics.

1889   Nietzsche, having declared "God is dead," succumbs to madness in Turin.

1921   Wittgenstein publishes *Tractatus Logico-Philosophicus*, claiming the "final solution" to the problems of philosophy.

1920s   Vienna Circle propounds Logical Positivism.

1927   Heidegger publishes *Being and Time*, heralding split between analytical and Continental philosophy.

1943   Sartre publishes *Being and Nothingness*, advancing

Heidegger's thought and instigating existentialism.

1953   Posthumous publication of Wittgenstein's *Philosophical Investigations*. High era of linguistic analysis.

Chronology of Leibniz's Life

1646	Born at Leipzig (in modern eastern Germany).
1652	Death of father.
1661	Enters Leipzig University to study law at age fourteen.
1666	Refused doctor of law degree at Leipzig on account of age. Takes doctorate at Altdorf University, Nuremberg.
1667	Takes appointment at court of Archbishop of Mainz.
1672	Sent to Paris on diplomatic mission to court of Louis XIV.

1675	Final development of his advanced calculating machine. Discovers mathematical calculus (unaware of Newton's prior discovery).
1676	Accepts post at the court of the Duke of Hanover. Visits Spinoza in Holland on roundabout journey to take up position at Hanover.
1680	Old Duke of Hanover dies and is succeeded by his brother, who has ambitions to become Elector of Hanover.
1685	Leibniz ordered to research history of the House of Hanover, with aim of securing electorship of the duke.
1692	Duke of Hanover becomes Elector, largely as a result of Leibniz's efforts.
1698	Elector of Hanover dies and is succeeded by his unsympathetic son, George.

78

1700	Leibniz becomes first president of the new Prussian Academy of Sciences, which he did so much to found.
1714	Elector of Hanover succeeds to throne of England and travels to London, leaving Leibniz behind. Leibniz eventually publishes *Monadology,* which outlines his metaphysical system.
1716	Dies at Hanover.

Recommended Reading

E. J. Aiton, *Leibniz: A Biography* (Hilger, 1985). This is the only full-scale biography in English of Leibniz's extremely varied life. Worth searching for in university and specialist libraries.

Nicholas Jolley, ed., *The Cambridge Companion to Leibniz* (Cambridge University Press, 1994). Essays for nonspecialist readers by experts in various aspects of Leibniz's philosophy.

Gottfried Wilhelm Leibniz, *Philosophical Papers and Letters* (Kluwer, 1976). By far the best selection of Leibniz's voluminous papers, many of which remained in his trunk until long after his death.

Gottfried Wilhelm Leibniz, *Philosophical Writings*, G. H. R. Parkinson, ed. (Everyman, 1990). Well-chosen selections from his major writings and letters, including the *Monadology*.

Bertrand Russell, *A Critical Exposition of the Philosophy of Leibniz* (Routledge, 1993). This classic work remains the most insightful, if the most controversial, critique of Leibniz.

Index

A NOTE ON THE AUTHOR

Paul Strathern has lectured in philosophy and mathematics and now lives and writes in London. A Somerset Maugham prize winner, he is also the author of books on history and travel as well as five novels. His articles have appeared in a great many publications, including the *Observer* (London) and the *Irish Times*. His own degree in philosophy was earned at Trinity College, Dublin.